CLEAR COACHING

Harness Clarity To Drive Development

Todd Beane

GRATITUDE

To a remarkable woman and six children,

To a courageous sister and a caring brother,

To friends from Tahoe to Catalonia,

To my parents above,

I am grateful.

WISDOM

We must always seek joy and inspiration as much in training as in competition.

Johan Cruyff

CONTENTS

4 STEPS TO CLEAR COACHING

1

Detail Your WHY
Clarity of Purpose

2

Define the Ideal
Clarity of Expectations

3

Train the Ideal
Clarity of Action

4

Model the Ideal
Clarity of Leadership

ONLY EXTRAORDINARY WILL DO

Welcome.

I feel compelled to present a bit of poetic balance to the practical nature of this book. I do so because I believe that to be an educator is to be both an artist and a scientist. I believe our craft begs us to see the boundless potential in our children.

Boundless. This is the potential we have to enact change.
Profound. This is the type of change it will require.
Resounding. This is the success we will have.

I hear these concepts whistle like wind through my imagination. Boundless potential, profound change, resounding success. Boundless, profound, resounding.

But wind is just that. It stirs. It fades. A few will be knocked off-kilter and a few will set sail to escape, but most will remain steadfast and stubborn in the comfort of mediocrity.

I know. For far too long, I have remained mediocre at many things because I did not heed the call to do more, to do better, to progress. I did not learn that last language, delve deeper into that last relationship, and challenge that last assumption.

But then I did.

I chose to unravel those assumptions. I chose to listen to a sage. I chose to make sense of that discontent nestled in my gut. I took notes. And when the breeze asked me to sway from my obstinacy, I leaned deeper into what might be and let go of what has always been.

How many of us cling to the common when common sense asks us to think differently?

When we need to redesign our approach do we? When we are encouraged to rethink our craft will we?

I have my doubts after hearing countless colleagues share their stories of deep frustration. Leaders who feel trapped by a system so anchored in the average that extraordinary appears a feeble zephyr. I have my doubts because these are good and capable people.

Doubt can lead to complicity, rationalization to submission, and indolence to apathy. And that is not acceptable for anyone who cares about children.

We do not have to have all the answers to catch the winds of change. We can set course for a new world on a flat earth. To do so, we must step from the shore on which the mundane has rooted.

Believe me, there will be chains that we must break. There will be people we must offend by our ambition. There will be those aiming to drown the voyage before it begins. To kill the messengers before they sing.

But mediocrity beckons boldness.

We are too adventurous to adhere to "the way it has always been." Just that paltry phrase should send us screaming. We know too much to teach the way we were taught. We are too intelligent to perpetuate poor pedagogical practices.

We will bless the breeze and let it move us.

We will inquire.

We will listen.

We will research and read.

We will discover and learn.

We will innovate and execute.

We will err and evaluate.

We will collaborate and celebrate.

We are done with average. There is too much average out there already.

From this day forward, only extraordinary will do.

INTRODUCTION

Your Calling

You owe it to all of us to get on with what you're good at.

W.H. Auden

Teaching matters. Coaching matters. Furthermore, we know these endeavours depend upon capable leaders.

So what?

For most people, it ends there. However, for you it starts here.

You read voraciously and jot notes on napkins. You care about kids. You care about your craft. In fact, you are drawn deeply into this role that found you as much as you found it. For every ten moments of frustration, you are gifted one of inspiration, and that is enough for you.

You are an educator.

Why read this book?

He who is not impatient is not in love.

Proverb

If you are like me, you crave clarity.

If you are like me, you seek efficiency.

If you are like me, you want to bring forth the best in your students.

And if you share my flaw of impatience, you want to do that now.

I am not an expert. I merely repackage the amazing into the manageable. This book is designed for a proactive coach. If you are willing to reflect and to act, you will find this book useful.

This book is about clarity of purpose, clarity of expectations, clarity of action, and clarity of leadership.

It is based upon years of experience working with thousands of coaches and educators worldwide, but it is designed for you.

Will it work?

The single biggest problem in communication is the illusion that it has taken place.

George Bernard Shaw

Sometimes it works.

I have built a model that serves me well. It may be valuable to you. It may not. I can say that I present it with a sincere agenda.

I will share how to harness clarity to drive development. I am not even sure what that means. I just know that once I took the steps presented to you here my coaching improved tremendously.

This model shaped my purpose. It encouraged me to detail exactly what I was hoping to accomplish each day with my student-athletes. The process I share drove me from my baseline to better.

How is this book organized?

It takes as much energy to wish as it does to plan.

Eleanor Roosevelt

Reading will be the easy part.

I ask that you consider this a process.

I will present the steps, but you must take them. As with all coaching, I can only facilitate the activities and encourage you along the way. You must choose clarity. You must choose to commit to improving your performance.

You will begin by establishing your purpose and proceed to clarify your ideas and actions as an educator. In the end, you will have drawn your own roadmap to better, and better is a good place to be.

Step 1: Detail your WHY.

Step 2: Define the ideal.

Step 3: Train the ideal.

Step 4: Model the ideal.

My Apologies

Beware the man of a single book.

Thomas Aquinas

I am trying to speak to you through the words on a page. I cannot do that. I need to speak with you in odd phrases with poor punctuation. To the grammarians, I apologize in advance.

I am not an expert in much of anything, really. I construct my thoughts on the work of true scholars and accomplished researchers. Let me applaud those from whom I beg, borrow, and steal.

Else if you would be a man speak what you think today in words as hard as cannonballs, and tomorrow speak what to-morrow thinks in hard words again, though it contradicts everything you said today. Ralph Wald Emerson

And finally, let me present to you "today in words as hard as cannonballs" what I hope to be woefully inadequate in the future. There are few absolutes. You will need to embrace the innovation yet to come for the sake of the children yet to come. They deserve your continued commitment to learning.

Chapter Summary

1. This book is not perfect, but it may make you a better coach.

2. Coaching is a process of patience.

3. Strive for clarity of thought and action.

Detail Your WHY
Clarity of Purpose

Define the Ideal
Clarity of Expectations

Train the Ideal
Clarity of Action

Model the Ideal
Clarity of Leadership

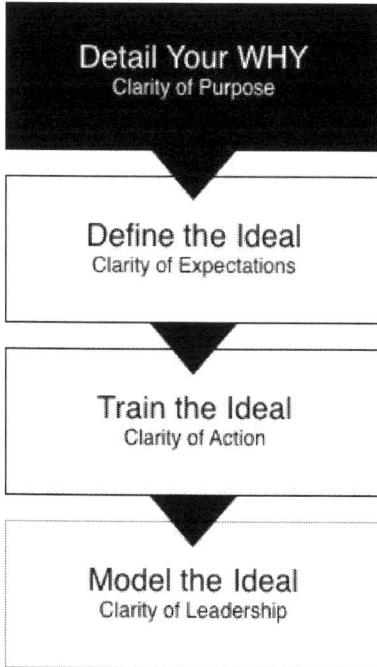

Clear Coaching Process

CLARITY OF PURPOSE

Step 1: Detail Your WHY

Why do you coach?
For whom do you coach?
What do you coach?

Why do you coach?

The discovery of WHY completely changed my view of the world.

Simon Sinek

Purpose is a powerful thing. Those who have it drive forward and those without it stray aimlessly seeking direction.

You are an educator and you have circled this concept of purpose for many years. However, circling is not pinpointing.

Circle: to revolve around
Pinpoint: to describe exactly

Specifying your motivation for coaching will serve you well on your journey.

Your WHY is your departure point, your focal point, and your destination all in one.

WORKSHOP EXERCISE

Why do you coach?
(Answer in one sentence.)

❇ ❇ ❇

For whom do you coach?

No man ever steps in the same river twice,
for it's not the same river and he's not the same man.

Heraclitus

Heraclitus' words are true for each of you. You have your identity, your story. No two coaches are identical in form or foundation. You get that. However, when I collect responses from coaches worldwide as to why they coach, a common voice emerges.

As if in harmony, coaches end up detailing for whom they coach.

Here are the most common responses from your colleagues worldwide.

I coach...

to instill passion in my players.
to provide an opportunity for my players.
to teach values to my players.
to promote joy for my players.

Passion, opportunity, values, and joy **for the players**. You, like so many, coach for the child in your charge.

The athlete is your departure point, your focal point, and your destination all in one.

What do you coach?

The future depends upon what you do today.

Mahatma Gandhi

Now on to WHAT.

WHAT is going to require a bit more work on your part. Before you advance, take a moment to consider the following.

WHY is about the purpose.

WHAT is about the product.

HOW is about the process.

The product is the result of your effort. Here, I do not refer to a match result. I refer to the result of your coaching. In sport, many believe wins and losses are the metrics that matter most. That may be accurate at the professional level. However, if you coach to provide opportunities, teach values, and promote joy, then the metrics must gauge whether or not you have achieved those objectives.

What will your work as a coach produce? Consider what you hope to nurture in your players.

Concise: brief in form but comprehensive in scope

Can you concisely articulate what a player must do, know, and be in order to excel? Brief and comprehensive. This is a powerful combination. Imagine that you have a clear rubric for excellence. Imagine that you specify your expectations and diligently prepare to train those mastery goals.

The next step is to add clarity of expectations to your clarity of purpose.

Chapter Summary

1. Your purpose will anchor you.

2. Your expectations will guide you.

3. Nurture each child in your charge.

Detail Your WHY
Clarity of Purpose

Define the Ideal
Clarity of Expectations

Train the Ideal
Clarity of Action

Model the Ideal
Clarity of Leadership

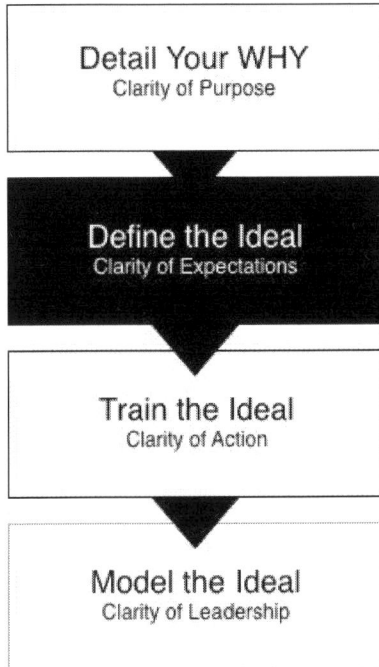

Clear Coaching Process

CLARITY OF EXPECTATIONS

Step 2: Define the Ideal

Where are you in the process?
Choose a destination.
Move from baseline to better.
Set high expectations.
Have faith.
Eliminate excuses.
Create a model.
Refine your model.
Share your model.

Where are you in the process?

Step 1: You have clarity of purpose. You have detailed your WHY.

Step 2: You will clarify expectations. You will define the ideal.

You articulated your motivation to coach. Now, you will construct a standard of excellence.

Choose a Destination

"Would you tell me, please, which way I ought to go from here?"

"That depends a good deal on where you want to get to," said the Cat.

"I don't much care where–" said Alice.
"Then it doesn't matter which way you go," said the Cat.

Lewis Carroll

Clear coaches define the ideal, and in doing so set a destination.

You realize that the time you have with a player is limited. You can run a training session and still run astray. Direction and destination matter.

This may seem obvious. However, it is often neglected. It is not specific enough to say that you are training to win. No coach sets out to lose. It is not focused enough to say that you want to develop players. No coach wants to stunt growth.

It matters where you want to go. The responsibility to choose a direction and a destination is yours. Specificity leads to clarity.

Move from Baseline to Better

We often gain awareness through a baseline comparison between now and next.

Sharon Weil

See the student before you. This provides you a snapshot of today. Also, see the student beyond you. This affords you a snapshot of tomorrow. Your role as an educator is to guide a child from baseline to better.

Now is a baseline. Next is better.

Each child arrives to you with a baseline of abilities; you have not had an influence on her development yet. Fair enough. However, on day one you are accountable for her development going forward. You are an agent of growth.

Let me alarm you with the following statement.

Athletes will learn with or without you.

This is quite a blow to your ego, I know. Mine, too. But why? You believe that a student will improve with your instruction. You believe that your coaching has a positive impact. You believe that you facilitate the maturation process.

I am not evaluating you; I am in no position to do so. However, your instruction is merely an intervention. You assume that your intervention adds value. But does it?

Now is a baseline.
Training is an intervention.
Next is better.

In other words, your intervention must achieve the expectations you determine.

What types of expectations should you set?

Set High Expectations

High achievement always takes place in the framework of high expectation.

Charles Kettering

In the 1960s Harvard Psychologist Robert Rosenthal teamed up with Lenore Jacobson, an elementary school principal. They embarked upon a study to examine the effects of expectations on student performance. In doing so, these two pioneers opened a debate on how expectations drive student performance.

Fast forward.

In 2019 researchers Olivia Johnston, Helen Wildy, and Jennifer Shand reviewed a decade of research on this topic and came to the following conclusion.

Students are likely to be affected by what their teachers expect of them. Educational research about teacher expectations has illustrated this relationship over the last century and more than 50 years of research. Johnston, Wildy & Shand

When you set high standards for your athletes, you do so for yourself as an educator as well. There is a double benefit. Both you and the athlete will accomplish more when you expect more. The research is clear on this issue.

Stephen Covey put forth a ground-breaking book, *7 Habits of Highly Successful People*. He sold over twenty-five million copies in forty different languages. Covey, an engaging speaker, traveled the world to inspire people to maximize their full potential. In essence, he became a global coach. He eloquently sums up the relationship between expectation and human potential.

Treat a man as he is and he will remain as he is. Treat a man as he can and should be and he will become as he can and should be. Stephen Covey

The expectations you set matter. The faith you have in your player matters.

Have Faith

It always seems impossible until it is done.

Nelson Mandela

Beyond sport.

In 2019, an artist from Lafayette, Louisiana walked on stage to receive a Grammy Award. Lauren Daigle's song, *You Say*, was inspired by her Christian faith and speaks volumes about the power of belief.

Lauren was fifteen years old when she was diagnosed with cytomegalovirus. This immune deficiency kept her out of school for two-years. During this time, Lauren's mother thought voice lessons would keep her daughter from depression.

Lauren herself best explains, "What you think might overwhelm you, is just the beginning."

I relaxed one morning listening to Lauren's song in which she sings to this power of belief. I felt that each student I have ever taught and each player I have ever coached needed me to believe in them. Faith is not the exclusive domain of religion. It is not merely a song. Faith resides in each word you utter to an athlete.

You may recognize the tremendous role you play in setting expectations. If you have faith in your players, you give them every opportunity to thrive. You are an adult, and what you believe about a child and what you say to them is significant.

Your athlete believes you.

Eliminate Excuses

He that is good for making excuses is seldom good for anything else.

Benjamin Franklin

Perhaps you have an excuse suggesting that your kids cannot possibly accomplish **X**, because they are merely **Y**. In your town, there are too few resources. In your club, there are too many barriers. On your team, there is not enough talent.

I can tell you that there is an excuse for every occasion. I have been fortunate to work with coaches from humble clubs to the world's best. There are remarkable coaches everywhere and at every level.

However, I have also been warned by at least one coach in each region that success is not an option. In Canada, it is too cold. In South Africa, it is too hot. In Costa Rica, it is too remote. You get the picture.

There are no shortages of justifications to lower expectations. You will hear them everywhere. The question is whether you choose to find excuses or to find solutions.

Create a Model

Our goals can only be reached through the vehicle of a plan. There is no other route to success.

Pablo Picasso

Imagine a name like this.

Pablo Diego José Francisco de Paula Juan Nepomuceno María de los Remedios Cipriano de la Santísima Trinidad Ruíz y Picasso.

It is no wonder that we know him merely as Pablo Picasso.

Born in Malaga, Spain in 1881, Pablo began drawing as a child but was far from exceptional in traditional school. With passion and persistence, Picasso became an artist known worldwide for his creativity and skill.

In describing his exploration into varied themes and forms, Picasso explained that it "is a matter of following the idea one wants to express and the way in which one wants to express it."

Picasso literally painted his vision. His goals were "reached through the vehicle of a plan." Furthermore, his mother seemed to understand the full potential of the child before her. She seemed to see now to next, baseline to better.

When I was a child, my mother said to me, 'If you become a soldier, you'll be a general. If you become a monk you'll end up as the pope,'" he later recalled. "Instead, I became a painter and wound up as Picasso. Pablo Picasso

I share this because we often fail to recognize that mastery and creativity come from structure. And while you may not be an artist, you are painting a picture.

What is the idea you want to express?

As a coach, you have in mind what you believe to be a brilliant athlete, a capable athlete, an admirable athlete. You may not have taken the time to put the idea to canvas yet, however, you have a vision of the ideal.

If your vision is not clearly expressed, it has no chance of being realized.

If your vision is as long as Pablo Picasso's entire name, it has no chance of being remembered. Create a clear vision. Create a concise model. Do so for yourself and your players.

Here are a few questions to clarify your vision.

What does a player need to do?

What does a player need to know?

What does a player need to be?

WORKSHOP EXERCISE

List the traits of an ideal player.

❊ ❊ ❊

Refine Your Model

True refinement seeks simplicity.

Bruce Lee

Pruning is painful.

Pruning is also productive.

Your list of an ideal athlete will be too long. I have asked you to list the infinite. There are so many qualities required to be exceptional.

Look back at your list.

How many traits detail specific skills?

For example, the ability to...

strike
throw
receive
pass
catch
shoot
block
skate

How many traits detail a sense of intelligence?

For example, the ability to...

perceive
create
conceive
make decisions
envision
read the game
anticipate
assess

How many traits detail character?

For example, qualities such as...

ambitious
dedicated
respectful
humble
positive
reflective
disciplined
loyal
reliable

You may find that your list includes more traits associated with character than with skill. If so, you are not
alone. You may also note that your list includes too
many items.

Prune.

As painful as pruning might be, it is also productive. As
Bruce Lee suggests, "True refinement seeks simplicity."
So do your players. If you can articulate this vision by
memory, or on a napkin, you are on the right path. If
you can sketch it, even better.

Make your vision manageable by making it concise.
Make your vision memorable by making it visual.

Take time now to refine your list.

Share Your Model

Few, if any, forces in human affairs are as powerful as a shared vision.

Peter Senge

You have what you need within you.

As I mentioned, you are an educator and you have circled these concepts of purpose and product for many years. However, now you are pinpointing. You describe with precision your WHY and your WHAT.

WHY is about the purpose. You have crafted a sentence to clarify your calling.

WHAT is about the product. You have created a model to clarify the ideal.

There is still work to be done, but review what you have accomplished thus far. You are harnessing clarity to drive development one step at a time. Well done.

As Rosabeth Moss Kanter of Harvard Business School states, "A vision is not just a **picture** of what could be, it is an **appeal** to our better selves, a **call** to become something more."

A *picture* is an image. An *appeal* is an earnest request. A *call* is a shout. When you share your vision with a player you are presenting an image of the ideal, requesting her to journey with you to that ideal, and giving your ideal a voice.

Share your model.

Publish it, post it, and present it. Give it form and shout it out. Your player needs to see it, to understand it, and even contribute ideas to it. Be direct about how this model will guide your coaching.

You have created a pact with your player. Why you train, for whom you train, and what you train is woven into that promise.

Now it's time to clarify HOW you will train.

Chapter Summary

1. Set a clear destination.

2. Intervene wisely.

3. Expect to achieve.

4. Show faith in your players.

5. Find solutions, not excuses.

6. Express a clear and compelling vision.

7. Create a memorable model.

8. Present your model as a promise.

Detail Your WHY
Clarity of Purpose

Define the Ideal
Clarity of Expectations

Train the Ideal
Clarity of Action

Model the Ideal
Clarity of Leadership

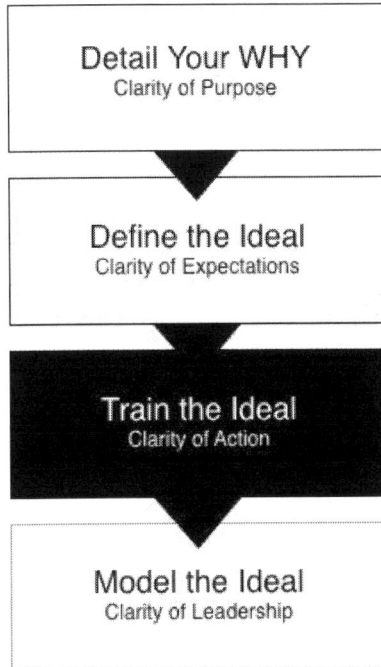

Clear Coaching
Process

CLARITY OF ACTION

Step 3: Train the Ideal

Where are you in the process?
Frame the journey.
Note the baseline.
Envision the ideal.
Mind the gap.
Design for learning.
Prune and prepare.
Train holistically.
Establish routines.
Let it go.

Where Are You In The Process?

Step 1: You have clarity of purpose. You have detailed your WHY.

Step 2: You have clarity of expectations. You have defined the ideal.

Step 3: You will develop clarity of action by training the ideal.

You are exploring how to harness clarity to drive development. This is not a complex process. In fact, it is a simple formula. However, I can tell you from professional experience that very few coaches and fewer organizations have taken the steps you are completing. I share this to applaud your patience and to encourage you to remain resolute in the tasks ahead.

Frame the journey.

Simplicity is the ultimate sophistication.

Leonardo da Vinci

The hero's story is one told throughout the ages. A protagonist of courage and ambition, like Homer's Odysseus, journeys through trial to triumph.

Fast forward.

A premature baby is born in Saint Bethlehem, Tennessee in 1940. Diseased and crippled in childhood, Wilma Rudolph goes on to become the first American woman to win three gold medals in a single Olympiad in Rome in 1960.

The hero's journey resonates deeply as it is the journey of potential unleashed, a vision realized. It is a story of human triumph.

As a coach, this journey is one you frame for the athlete. You begin with the baseline, however humble it may be. You set the ideal, however ambitious that may be. Then you bridge the gap.

It is a simple story, but the learning journey is one of great sophistication and significance.

The Learning Journey

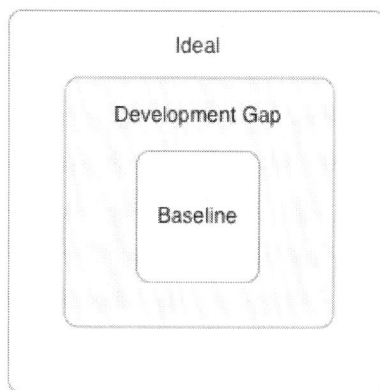

A **baseline** is a specific value that serves as a comparison. A baseline represents today. It represents an athlete's current ability. A baseline is your departure point, a child on day one looking to you primed with potential.

A **development gap** is an opportunity for growth. A development gap represents the time between now and the future. It represents the acquisition of knowledge, skills, and character. The gap is a training zone; a child fully engaged in learning.

An **ideal** is a standard of excellence. An ideal represents the future. It represents an athlete's expanded set of skills. An ideal is your destination, a child better prepared.

Seen in this light, your task becomes quite clear.

You will educate an athlete. You will bridge the gap between now and the future with positive reinforcement and refinement.

We want to help our players make the connection with their potential until it becomes real for them. Pete Carroll

Let's tackle these three elements in the following order.

Note the baseline.
Envision the ideal.
Mind the gap.

Note the baseline.

Not everything that can be counted counts, and not everything that counts can be counted.

William Bruce Cameron

Understand the athlete before you today.

Be careful as you assess the baseline qualities of an individual. Keep in mind that numbers are not a person. Also, understand that you harbor bias and that bias bleeds into every observation you make evaluating the qualities of other human beings. The research on this is clear.

The point here is that children are complex and remarkable beings. They develop better with advocacy than with negative scrutiny. Do not obsess over analytics to the point that a child feels like she is playing sport under a microscope.

Stay true to your noble purpose of promoting learning. As you do, responsibly observe and collect pertinent information. You are attempting to take a snapshot of today.

Knowledge: What does your athlete know today?

Skills: What can your athlete do today?

Character: How does your athlete behave today?

Take note of the knowledge, skills, and character you have listed on the ideal athlete model. You will want to collect specific data that is aligned with those characteristics. There are many ways this can be done.

Athlete Survey
Ask the athlete. Why is she participating? What are her goals? What would she like to improve? What part of her character brings pride? What does she expect from you?

Parent Survey
Ask the parents. What are their expectations? What are their priorities? What background information will support the development of their child?

Physical Metrics
Conduct tests. Of course, here it is important to make the distinction between what a player can control and

what is beyond his control. For example, a player does not control his height, maturation schedule, or birth month. Do not prejudice a child for factors beyond his control.

Video

Record the training. Record the first day's exercises and return to that video to show a player her progress. Keep in mind that a player's motivation is fueled by a belief in progress. An athlete may not see her own improvement. If you document progress and praise a player's effort, the effect is profoundly powerful. Show and tell, so to speak.

Of course, your specific sport will have its own traditional and creative opportunities.

In clear coaching, you are trying to present a realistic assessment of today without burdening the athlete with negative scrutiny. You will use this information to document the change in your student over the time she spends with you.

There is another reason to collect baseline data. You have an obligation to facilitate improvement. You are also on a learning journey.

The baseline is the version of your athlete today. Note it.

Envision the ideal.

I never believed I could actually free climb El Cap in a day when I first set the goal for myself. It didn't seem like a realistic objective for me. I didn't have the skills, fitness, or risk profile to move so quickly over such a large piece of stone. But I chose it exactly for that reason. Impossible dreams challenge us to rise above who we are now to see if we can become better versions of ourselves.

Emily Harrington

On a cool November morning in 2020, Emily Harrington set out to accomplish what no other woman had ever achieved. Before her was the impressive and daunting face of El Capitan of Yosemite National Park in California. Emily shares her thoughts on the record-breaking feat she accomplished.

On Nov 4, I started climbing with Alex Honnold at 1:34am, caught between my own internal drama of achieving a life goal and the more prevalent one of the elections - both unfolding in parallel ways in my brain. I knew I was in for a big day - but that's exactly why I was there. I wanted to find my limit and exist in it and fight beyond it.

A nasty slip on the 13a Golden Desert pitch almost took my resolve - a deep gash on my forehead left me bloody and defeated. I pulled on again, part of me not really wanting to stay on the wall, the other part gathering courage and flow. I kept thinking "why am I still hanging on?"

The next pitch was the A5 traverse, where I failed last year. This time it was not my limit. I fought hard but with flawless movements in the dark. I cried at the belay - it could hap-

pen this time....The final 5 pitches felt scary in my current state but I pulled over the final lip at 10:30pm in disbelief.
Emily Harrington

Emily discovers a better version of herself. She reveals a resilience carved from self-doubt.

Your athlete may not be able to imagine the potential she has within her. As a coach, you often paint that image for a child before she can paint it for herself. You see in her that which is not yet realized.

I saw the angel in the marble and carved until I set him free.
Michelangelo

Look at your ideal athlete model. In some form, you have envisioned an intelligent player, a skillful player, and a respectful player. These words may not be exactly yours, but the agenda is clear. You have set the ideal, and in doing so set the destination.

Intelligence

Skill

Character

An ideal athlete **intelligently** meets the challenge.

An ideal athlete **skillfully** executes her sport.

An ideal athlete possesses the **character** to compete respectfully.

Use this as your focal point on both the macro and micro levels of planning. At the macro-level, direct all energy to facilitating growth over the course of an entire season. You see the future.

At the micro-level, direct all energy to facilitating progress today. You act now. The accumulation of effective micro-moments will lead to macro-level achievement.

The real is clear.
The ideal is clear.
The gap awaits.

Mind the gap.

What if my job as a coach is really to prove to these kids how good they already are, how good they can possibly become, and that they are truly capable of high-level performance?

Pete Carroll

Human potential is the gap between what is and what might be.

Your athlete comes to you as a product of nature and nurture. Any energy bemoaning the fact that your athlete is not perfect is wasted energy. A child stands before you and you begin at the baseline. You will never reach the ideal, but that does not deter you. Do not dwell on the baseline. Do not obsess about the ideal.

Mind the gap.

To be clear, the gap is not a deficiency. That is a negative connotation that fails to honor the child before you, and the abilities she has acquired already. The development gap is space available for progress. It is a positive zone. If you and the athlete see this space as human potential, then you will see it as a sweet spot. You both recognize the reality of now and move through the gap celebrating achievement.

Goals are about the results you want to achieve. Systems are about the processes that lead to those results. James Clear

Your training sessions fill that gap. Both the content of your program and the delivery of that program are critical to success. Clear coaching requires both a well-constructed and well-executed training program to bridge the development gap.

Design an effective training program.

Design for Learning

Learning is a permanent change in behaviour or knowledge. Performance is a temporary fluctuation in behaviour or knowledge which can be observed and measured during and immediately after acquisition.

Harry Fletcher Wood

Training is not learning; learning is learning.

Training is merely an intervention to promote learning.

It is worth repeating that learning is a permanent change in knowledge. Learning is a permanent change in know-how. Learning is a permanent change in behavior.

I confess. I have crammed for a test and "performed' well enough to get by on the day. Thus, I had the illusion of learning. However, two weeks later I could not execute solutions requiring that knowledge. I may have performed well. I did not learn.

I want to emphasize this point considerably.

If a child in your charge must learn, you must understand how they learn.

This may seem obvious. However, the fact that it is logical does not make it a priority for many coaches or the organizations that train them. Many coaches spend exponentially more time studying the tactical elements of team performance than they do studying strategies to promote learning.

Consider your story. In the licensing courses you attend, how many hours are designated to understanding how children learn? The tactics of team performance usually overshadow the tactics of human development.

Design for learning.

A Dutch Twist on Learning

The Dutch have an interesting way of saying this. In Holland, the word "leren" (to learn) is used for both the act of teaching and the act of learning. An educator does not teach something to a student. An educator "learns" something to a student. It originally struck me as odd. Now, I think it is brilliant. The essence of all coaching is learning.

Innate Curiosity
Children are curious.

This point is obvious to anyone who has raised children or works with them. Children learn by satiating curiosity. They touch everything and make a mess of a lot of things. If you have children you know these truths to be self-evident.

The child, making use of all that he finds around him, shapes himself for the future. Maria Montessori

Children are masters of exploration and that is a good thing in terms of a learning journey. They are meaning makers. Through action and response, children learn.

Building Prototypes
Children build prototypes.

Protos: first
Typos: mold, pattern

A child creates his *first mold* of the game. It may be primitive, but he soon refines it. Iteration upon iteration. This is the creative process at work. He makes minor adjustments as the game he plays starts to resemble the more sophisticated version he sees from older peers or professionals.

If you can allow this process to unfold, then you will be more effective. If your training exercises ask the players to make these *first* primitive *molds and patterns*, then you are constructing the game conceptually. You are reinforcing prototypes in their primitive nature and working toward the model you hope to play in the future.

Consider requiring your player to build basic prototypes of the game and to think his way through the iterations required to build more sophisticated models.

Avoid breaking your sport into unrecognizable parts.

If you ask an athlete to see relationships, you will be asking him to do what he does naturally. You will be asking the athlete to construct solutions.

Training activities that are self-regulating and self-evident will give your player pertinent feedback that he needs to seek out the skills and knowledge required to improve. Of course, you intervene to question, to correct, or to confirm what you observe.

Perception-Action Coupling
Children see and do.

Without delving deeply into volumes of research articles that will reinforce this concept, let it be clear that athletes pick up cues from an environment as they act within it. You can go down a rabbit hole debating the semantics, but the obvious remains. Reading the environment and executing within it is a natural process.

Geir Jordet, a professor at the Norwegian School of Sport Sciences, has spent years researching the relationship between perception and action. He provides some advice to consider.

Exercises should provide players with the ability to locate many sources of information under severe time constraints, inducing the same dynamics prevalent in the players' use of their visual perceptual systems representative of real-world match play. Geir Jordet

Researchers Fuhre and Saether suggest that you "should create as many situations as possible where the players must make decisions and appropriate technical choices, and by that develop perceptual-cognitive and technical skills."

If you break this matrimony between perception and action, you divorce the athlete from the requirements placed upon her in competition.

The Power of Context
Children learn in context.

con: together
text: to weave

Again, I state the obvious. A child is part of the environment in which she operates. An athlete who learns in context *weaves together* the knowledge, skills, and character to meet the challenge presented.

A swimmer negotiates the water, a footballer the field, and a basketball player the court. She also competes and cooperates with other players in that environment.

In team games, attackers and defenders have been identified as coadapting components of complex self-organizing systems whose continuous interactive behaviors are regulated by information from the relative positioning and timing of movements of teammates and opponents with respect to key task constraints. Davids, Araujo, Correia, and Vilar

You may run the risk of dismissing the importance of learning in context. In fact, the traditional training paradigm often extracts action from the context in which it is executed. Reconsider that approach for the sake of your athlete.

Modern coaches take things apart and put them back together again but that's anti-natural. Without our context, we are not what we are. Juanma Lillo

As you proceed to emphasize learning, remember that context is king.

On Learning
By no means is this an adequate list of the elements contributing to the learning process. This book is not an exploration into the depths of pedagogy. However, consider these concepts as you design your training.

An athlete is curious.
An athlete learns through trial and error.
An athlete learns through perception and action.
An athlete learns in context.

Prune and prepare.

When you become sufficiently expert in the state of the art, you stop picking ideas at random. You are thoughtful about how to select ideas and combine ideas.

Andrew Ng

From the infinite choose the effective.

Much of preparation is a process of triage. How can you be as effective as possible with so many activities available? Choose exercises that lead directly to your ideal characteristics. Select exercises that respect the learning process.

In the age of information abundance and overload, those that get ahead will be the folks that figure out what to leave out so that they can concentrate on what's really important.
Austin Kleon

You will want to check your HOW against your WHY and WHAT. This can be accomplished by asking one question.

Does your training align with your ideal athlete model?

There are complicated drills and intriguing gadgets to help you create complex training constructions. These are distractions to clear coaching. It is common to see coaches amass drills assuming that a collection of drills is a purposeful program. Avoid the temptation of believing that a collection of good equals great. It does not.

Complicated training is not learning. Learning is learning.

Prune: to remove anything considered superfluous

Pruning can be painfully difficult. It can also be wonderfully liberating.

Prepare: to get ready; to compose

Clarity is the most important thing. I compare clarity to pruning in gardening. You have to be confident about your vision. After that, you just have to put a lot of work in. Diane von Furstenberg

You are nurturing the whole athlete. If you believe that the ideal athlete is one who competes in context with intelligence, skill, and character then your mandate is clear. Your training should develop intelligence, skill, and character in context. Moreover, you will ensure that your training exercises respect holistic development.

Planning, like architecture, is an exercise in design. A stormy marriage of process and creativity. Where science and art collide. Peps Mccrea

You have a limited amount of time to interact with an athlete. Thus, you have a limited amount of time to affect change. Implement the most efficient program possible. I hope to impress upon you that any distraction from your purpose is a waste of energy. Any derailment from holistic development is a waste of time.

The best coaches prune.

The best coaches prepare.

The best coaches build dynamic, engaging, and practical training sessions.

Train holistically.

Games are the most elevated form of investigation.

Albert Einstein

Consider the totality of competition.

An athlete manages oneself, manages relationships, manages space, and manages tasks. To manage the variables within the environment requires vision, precision, and pace. This is not news to you. You understand that skill applied is prowess. Speed of thought leads to speed of action. The best athlete finds space and exploits space to her advantage.

So what?

You have a compelling mandate.

If an athlete must play in context under pressure then you train in context under pressure.

What we have discovered is that a key factor for an effective transfer from the training environment to reality is that the training program ensures 'Cognitive Fidelity', this is, it should faithfully represent the mental demands that happen in the real world. Daniel Gopher

Your training will be faithful to cognitive demands. Faithful to technical demands. Faithful to the physical and social demands of competition. Ultimately, your training will remain faithful to the harmonious marriage of these demands in real-time.

Your players will struggle initially. No worries. Learning is messy and arduous. The benefits will come. In fact, one benefit to training holistically is that your athlete will begin to see the patterns inherent in your specific sport.

In pretty much every area, a hallmark of expert perform-

ance is the ability to see patterns in collections of things that would seem random or confusing to people with less well-developed mental representations.

The best players recognize and respond to the patterns almost instantaneously, taking advantage of weaknesses or openings as soon as they appear. Anders Ericsson

The importance of respecting both the integrity of competition and the integrity of pedagogical principles cannot be understated. Training sessions should remain on point.

If I don't practice the way I should, then I won't play the way I know that I can. Ivan Lendl

By training holistically, you engage the athlete in a coherent program. From one exercise to the next, the athlete applies all of herself to a task. She sees the connection clearly.

Students who develop mastery goals are motivated by the actual learning experiences. Their rewards arise from the challenges of acquiring and applying new knowledge and skills. Glenn Whitman, Ian Kelleher

There are many temptations to stray. Avoid them. You are on a path to clear coaching and total training is your best approach to nurturing an understanding of the game.

It is one thing to work on the technical gestures and another to work on the "technique of understanding the game." Cesar Luis Menotti

Training holistically is intelligence training. Training in context is skill training. Training on the edge is character training.

To train the ideal, train holistically.

Establish routines.

You must think clearly with a disciplined mind, especially in regard to the most efficient and productive use of time and resources.

Bill Walsh

You have pruned and prepared a coherent program.

It is now time to consider the effect of routine on learning. Routine to a child is familiarity. Routine is security. From the moment a child is born, he thrives in environments that afford safety. The research is abundantly clear and the effects are profound. A child develops confidence knowing that there is a loving advocate to protect, nourish, and support him. These elements are vital to clear coaching as well.

Routine maximizes learning by providing a safe environment. The best coaches implement routines as reliable and caring advocates.

Routine also maximizes efficiency. The best coaches concisely and precisely implement a learner-centric program.

Having strong procedures and routines is one of the most important things you can do to support learning... Ensuring that students know how to do frequently recurring tasks well is a driver of focus and efficiency. Doug Lemov

Well-executed routines cement processes that build a culture. A routine does not speak, but it communicates powerfully and it resonates deeply.

Without digressing too far, let me explore this a bit. Humans are creatures of deeply embedded rhythms. We have an internal regulatory system of cycles, and respecting our biological routines enhances positive development and growth.

Rhythm: procedure with uniform recurrence

Your athlete is a creature wired for routine. Training routines build confidence, nurture positive relationships, and allow an athlete to self-regulate. There is a reason why sport psychologists worldwide help athletes establish routines.

Routine: A regular course of procedure

Routines nurture positive habits. Your athlete will respond to both the coherency of your program and the consistency of its implementation.

Habit formation is the process by which behavior becomes progressively more automatic through repetition. The more you repeat an activity, the more the structure of your brain changes to become efficient in that activity. James Clear

Consider the various ways that you can build routines into your training session.

Welcome Routine
Do you consistently welcome a player to training?

For example, at most football clubs in Europe, it is customary that players shake the hands of the coaches as they enter into the training environment. This small routine, one handshake at a time, establishes a culture of respect. In fact, I have been a guest at FC Barcelona training where the players extend that courtesy to anyone within that cultural bubble. This is not laborious; it is an automatic action upon arrival to the training grounds.

Initiation Routine
What is the signal indicating that the session has started?

Routines are not random; they are well defined and recurring. Set a consistent protocol that informs the athlete that he must be completely focused.

Training Routine
Do you have a training template that is familiar and consistent?

For example, a well-run training session flows with precision. The athlete knows the daily plan. Minutes of precious time are preserved.

Transition Routine

Is the athlete transitioning smoothly from one task to the next?

When a player understands the protocols, he transitions quickly from one activity to the next. Even a water break has a structure. Train, hydrate, train.

Closing Routine

How do you close training?

A closing routine instructs a player to conclude the formal activity, store all equipment, and execute a post-training hydration protocol.

Farewell Routine

How do you say goodbye?

You started your session with a positive welcome and you conclude with an individual or team ritual.

Efficient routines are valuable. The greater number of minutes you engage a player in the optimal learning zone, the more productive you are as an educator.

Let it go.

It's funny how some distance makes everything seem small,
And the fears that once controlled me can't get to me at all...

Let it go. Let it go!

Idina Menzel

While reflection is healthy, obsession is counterproductive.

You develop a coherent session with a clear focus and deliver it to the best of your ability.

You do so with clarity of purpose.
You do so with clarity of expectations.
You train the ideal.

Even with these critical elements aligned, you walk away frustrated on certain days and elated on others. You have highs and you have lows because you care. You feel emotionally connected to the children in your charge. You want to deliver a dynamic, engaging, and practical training session every day. However, perfect coaching is elusive.

Let it go. Today is done.

Time to tend to yourself. Time to tend to your loved ones. They, too, deserve the best of you.

WORKSHOP EXERCISE

Create a training session.

(Ensure each exercise requires an athlete to make
choices in context under pressure.)

❋ ❋ ❋

Chapter Summary

1. Frame learning as a journey.

2. Measure the baseline, but see the potential.

3. Fill the development gap by expanding a child's ability.

4. Prioritize learning.

5. Prepare to train intelligently.

6. Train holistically.

7. Establish productive routines to promote self-regulation.

8. Do your best and move on.

Detail Your WHY
Clarity of Purpose

Define the Ideal
Clarity of Expectations

Train the Ideal
Clarity of Action

Model the Ideal
Clarity of Leadership

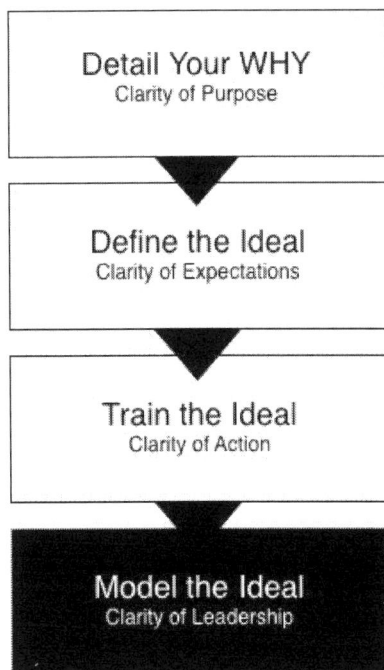

Clear Coaching
Process

CLARITY OF LEADERSHIP

Step 4: Model the Ideal

Where are you in the process?
Create a model.
Avoid a trap.
Refine your standards.
Execute with expertise.

Where are you in the process?

Step 1: Clarity of Purpose: You have detailed your WHY.

Step 2: Clarity of Expectations: You have defined the ideal.

Step 3: Clarity of Action: You train the ideal.

Step 4: Clarify Leadership. You will now model the ideal.

You matter.

What you say matters. What you do matters. How you behave sets a standard. As a mentor to children, you profoundly affect a child. This reality is both the beauty and the burden of leadership.

Not surprisingly, it is easier to set expectations for your athletes than for yourself. However, setting standards for yourself will provide you the clarity you need to lead.

Create a model.

It is a simple two-step process: Decide the type of person you want to be. Prove it to yourself with small wins. First, decide who you want to be. This holds at any level—as an individual, as a team, as a community, as a nation. What do you want to stand for? What are your principles and values? Who do you wish to become?

James Clear

What do you hope she says?

Imagine your player at the end of the season evaluating you. She is in the locker room speaking her mind. She evaluates your knowledge of the sport, your skills as an educator, and your character.

What does she actually say?

If you are a clear coach you transmit your knowledge and model the values you espouse. You are a caring coach if you nurture healthy relationships.

You have defined the ideal athlete which requires reflection. What about you? Do you have a rubric for yourself? Defining the ideal requires self-reflection. This is not an easy task nor is it a frivolous endeavor.

You are not the first to attempt it.

In 1726, a young man of twenty years of age set out to accomplish this task.

Benjamin Franklin, considered to be one of the Founding Fathers of the United States, was a politician, postmaster, printer, scientist, inventor, and writer among other trades. He explains the motivation for keeping a detailed record of his actions.

I conceived the bold and arduous project of arriving at moral perfection. I wished to live without committing any fault at any time; I would conquer all that either natural inclination, custom, or company might lead me into. As I knew, or thought I knew what was right or wrong, I did not see why I might not always do the one and avoid the other. But I soon found I had undertaken a task of more difficulty than I had imagined. Benjamin Franklin

Franklin goes on to detail thirteen virtues constituting his agenda.

1. Temperance
2. Silence
3. Order
4. Resolution
5. Frugality
6. Industry
7. Sincerity

8. Justice

9. Moderation

10. Cleanliness

11. Tranquility

12. Chastity

13. Humility

When you set out to define the ideal, you do not strive for mediocrity. You set lofty goals knowing your commitment will yield many benefits.

Franklin explains.

I entered upon the execution of this plan for self-examination, and continued it, with occasional intermissions, for some time. I was surprised to find myself so much fuller of faults than I had imagined; but I had the satisfaction of seeing them diminish. Benjamin Franklin

To be a clear coach is not to be a perfect coach; we know that to be impossible recognizing our human nature. Nonetheless, you demonstrate a commitment to growth. You are modeling exactly what you have asked your players to do. You, too, will define the ideal and train that ideal.

WORKSHOP EXERCISE

List the traits of an ideal coach.

* * *

Avoid a trap.

There are more important things in life than winning or losing a game.

Leo Messi

The trap awaits you.

Coaching is emotionally charged. You are either a winner or a loser. This is quite a harsh assessment when winning and losing are defined by score lines.

Let me explain.

Zero-sum Game Theory suggests that each participant's gain is equivalent to another's loss resulting in a sum of zero.

At first glance, sport may seem to be such. You may assume that only one coach can win. Don't. This is a false dichotomy. Clear and capable coaches can be on both benches, although one may win and one may lose on any given day.

In Step One, you established your purpose. Interestingly enough, most responses detailing WHY never mention trophies or championships. In fact, I am certain your WHY reinforces a commitment to your player's general well-being.

In Step Two, you defined your ideal athlete. Did you write *victorious* on that list? Your ideal list probably includes admirable traits. If you are like most coaches worldwide, you have many more words associated with character than a specific skill.

This begs us to consider the following.

Can you only promote learning and joy by winning games?

Can you only develop talent with a trophy in your hands?

Of course not. If you are moving players from baseline to better you can do this with strong or weak teams, in victory or defeat. The spoils of clear coaching are available to coaches up and down the standings table. Thankfully so. Imagine a world in which the learning and joy were portioned to the champions while the rest were conditioned to a worthless journey.

If we believe in a world in which we can feel inspired, safe, and fulfilled every single day and if we believe that leaders are the ones who can deliver on that vision, then it is our collective responsibility to find, guide, and support those who are committed to leading in a way that will more likely bring that vision to life. Simon Sinek

If you believe that inspiration is critical to a productive life, then it is your responsibility to provide that to your athletes. The good news is that you can inspire a child each day in training and in each competition.

You must avoid the trap of thinking that leading young people is a *Zero-Sum Game.* Your mentorship is so much more than a win or a loss. Your performance as a leader must be assessed by how closely you anchor to your purpose and how capably you guide players to the ideal.

Refine your standards.

I developed my Standard of Performance over three decades in the business of football.

Bill Walsh

If refining a model sounds like a familiar process, good.

In Step Two, you followed a similar process to refine the ideal athlete. Now we ask you to do the same to refine your ideal coach model.

To be a better coach is to be an evolving coach. Recognize that this will require iteration upon iteration. You, like the players, are on a learning journey.

Take a look at your list. Remember that pruning may be as painful as it is productive. Take the time to edit for simplicity.

How many traits detail specific knowledge?

How many traits detail certain skills?

How many traits detail character?

As in the case of depicting the ideal athlete, you may want to creatively represent your model. Ben Franklin went so far as to print out his rubric and to produce cards he used daily to register his performance.

A distinction.

I want to point out a significant distinction between defining the ideal athlete and defining the ideal coach. While both you and your athlete are committed to the sport, your tasks are different. You are a leader of young people. You are an adult. You are the educator who facilitates an athlete's positive development.

Your athlete is learning.

You are learning to educate.

This may seem obvious, but many coaches think that they are coaching a sport. In reality, you are mentoring a child and bringing your best to that task.

Tidy up your ideal coach model. Make your vision manageable by making it concise. Make your vision memorable by making it visual.

Take the time to refine your list.

Execute with expertise.

Our chief want in life is somebody who will make us do what we can.

Ralph Waldo Emerson

You control your efficacy as an educator.

Good coaching requires more than experience, it requires expertise. This is an important distinction. *Experience* you gain by working as time passes. *Expertise* you gain by honing your skills.

John Hattie, author of *Visible Learning for Teachers*, has done extensive research in the field of education. John explains that expert teachers...

1. Have high levels of understanding of the subject.

2. Can guide learning to desirable surface and deep outcomes.

3. Can successfully monitor learning and provide feedback that assists students to progress.

4. Can attend to the more attitudinal attributes of learning.

5. Can provide defensible evidence of positive impacts of the teaching on student learning.

Expert teachers have both knowledge and know-how. Expert teachers guide learning and measure it.

The evidence of your expertise rests in your athlete's improvement.

Chapter Summary

1. Set personal standards so that you may lead by example.

2. Redefine winning as promoting learning and joy.

3. Acquire knowledge of your sport.

4. Develop expertise as an educator.

5. Measure your athlete's progress and celebrate it.

CONCLUSION

It's what you learn after you know it all that counts.

John Wooden

I end where I began.

I find that arguments tend to be circular in nature. Most arguments are opinions couched in content and presented with purpose. With this in mind, let me return to my initial thoughts.

The first set of statements I assume about you:

You care.
You seek efficiency.
You want to bring forth the best in a child.
You want to do that now.

The second set of statements I share about me:

I am not an expert.
I have built a framework that serves me well.
I present it with a sincere agenda.
Sometimes it works.
It may be valuable to you. It may not.

Proposition: the act of offering something to be considered.

I propose that harnessing clarity drives development.

I argue that you and your athletes benefit from clarity of purpose, clarity of expectations, clarity of action, and clarity of leadership.

I go on to suggest that clarity is achieved by detailing your WHY, defining the ideal, training the ideal, and modeling the ideal.

Fair enough.

However, this is not necessarily true. This is not an absolute. As I mentioned previously, I merely repackage the amazing into the manageable. I beg, borrow, and steal wisdom from the sages. Women and men of philosophy, art, and education are my coaches.

I can say for certain that this argument does not address all that is coaching.

You and the athlete before you are the entirety of coaching.

In you rests passion.

In the child rests hope.

That is enough.

I wish you the best on your journey to extraordinary.

A CHILD'S PLAY

That you are here—that life exists and identity, That the powerful play goes on, and you may contribute a verse.

Walt Whitman

A parent will understand.

"What part do you play, Tali?" I ask.

"A tree," she responds.

"What do you do?"

"I stand, I sing, I fall," she explains.

I knew then that little Natalia had summed up my entire life as she buckled up in the backseat. I think she may have summed up humanity in her first role on a primary school stage.

"I stand, I sing, I fall."

If we are lucky, this is enough. If we are fortunate, we do this passion and perspective.

I stand.

I want so much that Tali finds her legs. That she takes her first steps of autonomy from a foundation we call home. To many, this may seem mundane. However, how many walk this earth upright without standing. Standing for personal and collective justice. Standing poised to voice our deepest hopes. Standing to embrace the life afforded to us.

I sing.

Tali will find her voice. It will not be mine. It will resonate from deep within her chords, and it will inspire her before it vibrates beyond. So simple, some may say. Just stand and sing. And yet, how many remain silent. A whisper works. A voice need not be loud to be heard, but it needs to take form from hope. That voice must be tuned to the instrument of a positive life.

I fall.

To each her fate. My Tali will falter and will feel the pain of doing so. There are a million moments of angst before the final fall. Since she does not yet understand the difference between Tuesday and May, I hope eternity can wait.

"I sing. I stand. I fall."

A parent will understand how much I want to direct this play realizing that I cannot, and knowing that I should not. I am a father first and a coach by profession, and, perhaps, these are one and the same. By post and profession, I am responsible for setting a stage for another's poignant performance.

As a coach, my task is to guide a young person as they stand and sing. My job is not to be the protagonist of my player's performance. My role is to create the optimal conditions in which a child may stand and sing through sport. My responsibility is to pick up a few emotional pieces after a fall. My task is to demonstrate that a win is to be celebrated and a loss to be a lesson.

As I look in the rear-view mirror on the road home from school, I see the years behind me, and a little girl that understands her role perfectly. She will stand tall, sing her tune, and fall to close the curtain on a child's play.

SUMMARY OF STEPS

1

Detail your WHY.
Clarity of Purpose

Determine why you coach.
Remember for whom you coach.
Promote learning and joy.

2

Define the ideal.
Clarity of Expectations

Choose a destination.
Move from baseline to better.
Set high expectations.
Have faith.
Eliminate excuses.
Create a model.
Refine your model.
Share your model.

3

Train the ideal.

Frame the journey.
Note the baseline.
Envision the ideal.
Mind the gap.
Design for learning.
Prune and prepare.
Train holistically.
Establish routines.
Let it go.

4

Model the ideal.

Create a model.
Refine your standards.
Execute with expertise.

RESOURCES

You have a wealth of authors, researchers, and colleagues beside you on your learning journey.

Recommended Authors & Books

Doug Lemov, Practice Perfect
John O'Sullivan, Every Moment Matters
Peps Mccrea, Motivated Teaching
Johan Cruyff, My Turn.
Bill Walsh, The Score Takes Care of Itself.
Pete Carroll, Win Forever.
James Clear, Atomic Habits.
John Hattie, Visible Learning for Teachers.
Mark Williams and Robin Jackson, Anticipation and Decision Making in Sport
Glenn Whitman and Ian Kelleher, Neuro Teach
Benjamin Franklin, Franklin's Autobiography: Eclectic English Classics
Simon Sinek, Start with Why and The Infinite Game.
Rinus Michels, Teambuilding.
Benedict Carey, How We Learn.
John Medina, Brain Rules
Cal Newport, Deep Work.
Peter Brown & Henry Roediger and Mark McDaniel, Make it Stick.
Daniel Kahneman, Thinking Fast and Slow.
Anders Ericsson & Robert Pool, Peak: The Secrets from the New Science of Expertise
Mark Williams and Tim Wigmore, The Best: How Elite Athletes Are Made
Daniel T. Willingham, Why Don't Students Like School?
Barbara Oakley and Terrence Sejnowski, Learning How to Learn
Ellen J. Langer, The Power of Mindful Learning
James Lang, Small Teaching
Shawn Anchor, The Happiness Advantage

Research Notes

A Practical Introduction
W.H. Auden, *Poet*
George Bernard Shaw, *Playwright*
Eleanor Roosevelt, *Diplomat & Activist*
Thomas Aquinas, *Philosopher*
Ralph Waldo Emerson, *Essayist & Poet*

Clarity of Purpose
Simon Sinek, *Start with WHY.*
Mahatma Ghandi, *Leader*

Clarity of Expectations
Lewis Carroll, *Alice's Adventures in Wonderland*
Sharon Weil, *Author*
Charles Kettering, *Engineer*
Robert Rosenthal & Lenore Jacobson, *Pygmalion in the Classroom*
Johnston & Wildy & Shand, *A decade of teacher expectations research 2008-2018.*
Stephen Covey, *Author*
Nelson Mandela, *Leader*
Lauren Daigle, *Interview on Z100 New York April 16,2019.*
Benjamin Franklin, *Author & Politician*
Pablo Picasso, *Artist information from Biography.com*
Bruce Lee, *Martial Artist*
Peter Senge, *Author*
Rosabeth M. Kanter, *Professor at Harvard Business School*

Clarity of Action
Leonardo da Vinci, *Artist*
Pete Carroll, *Winning Forever*
William Bruce Cameron, *Author*
Emily Harington, *Instagram. @emilyaharrington*
Michelangelo, *Artist*
Pete Carroll, *American Football Coach*
James Clear, *Atomic Habits*
Harry Fletcher Wood, *Responsive Teaching: Cognitive Science and Formative Assessment in*

Practice

Maria Montessori, *Educator*

Geir Jordet PhD, *geirjordet.com*

Jan Fuhre and Stig Arve Saether, *Skill acquisition in a professional and non-professional U16 football team: the use of playing form versus training form.*

Davids, Araujo, Correia and Vilar, *How Small-Sided and Conditioned Games Enhance Acquisition of Movement and Decision-Making Skills*

Juanma Lillo, *Football Coach*

Andrew Ng, *Businessman*

Austin Kleon, *Steal Like an Artist*

Diane von Furstenberg, *Fashion Designer*

Peps Mccrea, *Lean Lesson Planning*

Albert Einstein, *Scientist*

Daniel Gopher, *Technion-Israel Institute of Technology*

Anders Ericsson & Robert Pool, *Peak: Secrets from the New Science of Expertise*

Ivan Lendl, *Tennis Player*

Glenn Whitman, Ian Kelleher, Neuroteach: *Brain Science and the Future of Education*

Cesar Luis Menotti, *Football Manager*

Bill Walsh, *The Score Takes Care of Itself*

Doug Lemov, *Teach Like a Champion*

James Clear, *Atomic Habits*

Indina Menziel, *Let it Go*

Clarity of Leadership

James Clear, *Atomic Habits*

Benjamin Franklin, *Franklin's Autobiography: Eclectic English Classics*

Leo Messi, *Footballer*

Simon Sinek, *The Infinite Game*

Bill Walsh, *American Football Coach*

Ralph Waldo Emerson, *Essayist*

John Hattie, *Visible Learning for Teachers*

John Wooden, *Basketball Coach*

WORKSHOP SAMPLES

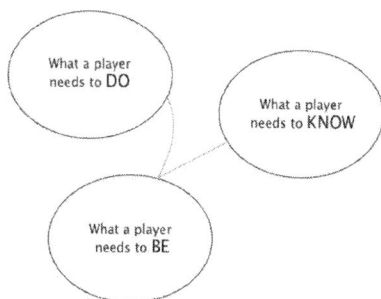

Ideal Athlete Workshop
Brainstorming Sample #1

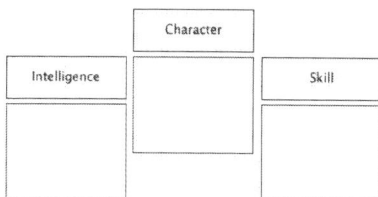

Ideal Athlete Workshop
Brainstorming Sample #2

PERSPECTIVE

This is a wonderful day.
I've never seen this one before.

Maya Angelou

ABOUT THE AUTHOR

Todd Beane

SHORT VERSION
Todd is lucky to spend his life doing what he loves.

PROFESSIONAL VERSION
Todd Beane educates athletes and coaches worldwide. He is the founder of TOVO Academy Barcelona and TOVO Institute.

He attended Dartmouth College, the University of Sussex, and Stanford University, finalizing his studies with a Master of Arts in Education.

Beane began teaching at Salisbury School, joined the faculty of Johns Hopkins University as Director of the Native Vision Program, and served as Director of the Cloud Forest School in Costa Rica.

In Europe, Beane was the Founding Director of the Cruyff Institute. Working with Johan Cruyff for over a decade, he created development programs for Ajax Amsterdam, Mamelodi Sundowns, Chivas Guadalajara, and FC Barcelona.

CONNECT

Todd Beane

Twitter: @_ToddBeane

Email: tb@tovoacademy.com

Website: www.tovoinstitute.com

FAREWELL

Dear Reader,

You can find me on the shores of the Mediterranean Sea in a village just south of Barcelona. I am an aging dog kept young by my own six children, and by the remarkable athletes in my charge.

For me, this book is more than a light read on coaching. It is about being a mentor. It is about realizing the potential of a child.

Talent development comes in many forms and is usually more meaningful when there is a capable educator like you working some magic.

Thank you for all that you do.

Sincerely,

Todd Beane

Printed in Great Britain
by Amazon